Stanley the Sleuth Uncovers the Story of Casimir Pulaski

written by
Rochelle A. Carman

illustrated by
Karen Berry Finn

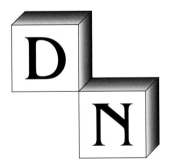

DanNiall Publishing
P.O. Box 92291
Elk Grove Village, IL 60009-2291

Stanley the Sleuth Uncovers the Story of
Casimir Pulaski

written by Rochelle A. Carman

illustrated by Karen Berry Finn

Published by:

DanNiall Publishing

P.O. Box 92291

Elk Grove Village, IL 60009-2291

U.S.A.

Library of Congress Catalog Card Number: 94-93853

Carman, Rochelle A.
Stanley the Sleuth Uncovers the Story of Casimir Pulaski

ISBN 1-886325-18-9 $14.95 hardcover

I go by the nickname of Stanley the Sleuth,
And I love to investigate.
I'm a seeker of knowledge, a finder of truth.
I'm quite famous although I'm just eight.

I read lots of books, and I ask lots of questions,
But some people think I'm a pest.
'Cause I want to know who, and I want to know why,
They say, "Stanley, please, give it a rest."

They say, "Give it up, Stanley,
This yackity-yacky.
Forget all your questions.
You're driving us wacky!"

But no one can stop me,
A kid on a quest,
'Cause I find what I seek,
And that's why I'm the best.

There once was this case where I saw a strange name,
An odd name on a calendar page.
"Casimir Pulaski"—I had to know more.
Was he poet or statesman or sage?

My mother was busily washing the dishes
When I had decided to try.
I asked her, "Who is this man named Pulaski?"
But she only turned with a sigh.

She said, "Give it up, Stanley,
This yackity-yacky.
Forget all your questions.
You're driving me wacky!"

"You can't try to stop me,
A kid on a quest,
'Cause I find what I seek,
And that's why I'm the best."

"Stanley," she said, "this is all I remember.
He's Polish and fought in some war.
He was a good soldier—a general, perhaps,
Who had won many battles before.

"Yes, the war against England, I think that was it,
When this Casimir Pulaski had fought.
He knew Benjamin Franklin and Washington, too.
Or at least that is what I had thought."

Mom turned to her dishes, and I realized
That she didn't have much more to say.
I'd have to decide upon some other plan,
And I'd still have to wait one more day.

Next, I went to my teacher, as I often do,
Just to pester him for some more help.
"Who's Casimir Pulaski?" I wanted to know.
But then he only started to yelp.

He said, "Give it up, Stanley,
This yackity-yacky.
Forget all your questions.
You're driving me wacky."

"Sir, you can't try to stop me,
A kid on a quest,
'Cause I find what I seek,
And that's why I'm the best."

"Well, all right Stanley, I'll tell what I know,
But the facts are not totally clear.
On the fourth day of March he was born long ago.
He grew up as a man without fear.

"He was a brave general who always rode
On his horses with daring and skill.
At a battle at Brandywine he helped us fight
With his cleverness and his strong will."

I couldn't believe that was all that he knew,
So I had to find out more myself.
I went to the library, looked at some books
From up high on the history shelf.

The librarian saw my discouraged expression,
And she asked me, "What is your task?"
I told her, "Oh, you really don't want to know.
Most adults hate the questions I ask."

"Don't give it up, Stanley—
Your yackity-yacky.
Don't give up your questions.
That *would* drive me wacky.

"Who'd want to stop you?
A kid on a quest.
'Cause you love to gain knowledge,
That's why you're the best."

(I had to grin.)

"I'm trying to learn about Casimir Pulaski.
It's harder than it might appear.
My mother and teacher know little at all,
And there isn't a single book here."

"Casimir Pulaski! Oh yes! This is great!"
And she led me to her big desk file.
"I've studied Pulaski for nearly a year.
I can help you," she said with a smile.

Two centuries passed since this hero was born,
Seventh child in his large family.
Though smaller and thinner, he always kept up.
He was proud as a young boy could be.

His family had many good books to read.
They had horses that they loved to ride.
Though Pulaski had some trouble learning at first,
He improved more each time that he tried.

As an adult with his father and brothers,
He fought to keep his country free.
They won many battles but still lost the war,
And from Poland they all had to flee.

He wrote to his country and asked to come home,
But no answer would ever come back.
Other men would give up, but not him, not a chance,
Though the future appeared to be black.

He heard of the Colonies' war against England,
And his hopes had started to soar.
He wrote to Ben Franklin and asked to help battle
For freedom and honor once more.

Ben talked to George Washington—told of his fame,
And then George was quite quick to agree,
"Let's hire this man who fought bravely in Poland—
This soldier of true liberty."

But Pulaski had problems. His horse was once injured.
Some soldiers were not pleased at first.
Yet he didn't lose hope. Yes, he worked out his problems,
Not quitting though things looked their worst.

The cavalry needed a great deal of training
And saddles and boots and more guns.
Pulaski, himself, bought supplies that they needed
Since Congress was so low on funds.

When the time came for battle, Pulaski looked out
At the cavalry in silent stand.
He promised to lead them with wisdom and courage.
They trusted Pulaski's command.

Some leaders in Charleston wanted to quit,
But Pulaski knew how to defend.
In Savannah his very last battle was fought,
For his life would be lost in the end.

He's remembered by many for starting his legion,
Those horsemen of brave dignity.
Because of his leadership, he is still known
As the "Father of Our Cavalry."

I thanked my friend for the things that she taught me,
Then thought of the story she told.
Pulaski had fought for the freedom of others,
So proud and so brave and so bold.

No one could stop him,
This man on a quest.
He would find what he'd seek.
That's why *he* was the best.

There was something about him that I really liked.
And I wondered, "Now what could it be?"
He always would try, and he never gave up.
Oh, yes, he was a little like me!

About the Author

Rochelle Carman is a free-lance writer. She is also a certified reading specialist and a veteran elementary school teacher. She earned her Master's in Education from National-Louis University in Evanston, Illinois. She enjoys spending time with her husband and son at their home in suburban Chicago.

About the Illustrator

Karen Berry Finn is a free-lance illustrator and artist. Her undergraduate work is from Eastern Illinois University, and her master's degree is from the School of the Art Institute in Chicago. She resides in Chicago with her husband and her new baby boy.

Events in Casimir Pulaski's Life

March 4, 1747—Casimir Pulaski is born in Warka, Poland on a large estate called Winiary. (There is some uncertainty as to the year of his birth, so 1746 and 1748 might also be found in history books.)

1752—He receives a pony from his father, Joseph, as a birthday gift. His father teaches him to ride expertly. His five older sisters, his older brother Francis, and his younger brother Anthony, are also taught how to ride.

1758—He goes to the School of the Teatine Order in Warsaw where he learns about music, art, and manners. While here, he earns only average grades, but he continues to practice his riding and marksmanship. He even learns how to shoot a bull's eye while on horseback.

1762—He goes to the palace of Prince Karl of Courland to learn to be an assistant to the prince.

1767—Now a young man, he gets his first experience with war. He and 200 of his fellow Poles break through 4,000 Russian soldiers encircling them in Courland.

1768—Joseph Pulaski, Casimir's father, organizes an army called the Bar Confederacy to defend Poland against the Russians. Casimir and his two brothers lead many battles. They learn a great deal about fighting and leadership.

1771—He becomes a national hero of Poland when he and his army overwhelmingly defeat Russian forces in Czestochowa, Poland.

1773—Russians defeat Pulaski's Bar Confederates. Francis dies in battle while Casimir, his father, and Anthony spend time in Prussian prisons. Later, his father dies in prison due to an epidemic. Casimir Pulaski is wrongly accused of a plot to kidnap and kill the king of Poland. When released from prison, Casimir flees first to Turkey where he tries to build an army to fight the Russians.

1776—Unsuccessful in Turkey and running out of money, he decides to go to France to find work. While in Paris he writes to the Polish authorities to ask to return to Poland, but he does not receive a response. He assumes that Polish officials still believe he plotted to kill the king. He is heartbroken that he is not allowed back into the country he loves.

November 1776—While in Paris, he learns more about the Revolutionary War in the New Land. Pulaski feels that the American fight for freedom from the British is much like his fight in Poland, and he wants to help. He writes Benjamin Franklin, who is in Paris at the same time, and asks him if he would consider hiring him to fight against the British.

June 1777—Thanks to a friend named Ruhleire and Pulaski's reputation in Europe for being a great war leader, Franklin decides to recommend Pulaski to George Washington. A Polish friend named Josef Zajeczek, along with Ruhleire and Silas Deane, help pay off his debts and pay for his passage to America.

July 23, 1777—He arrives in America and immediately sends a letter to George Washington to apply for a position in the Continental Army.

August 29, 1777—Washington knows that the Colonists have no trained cavalry, so he meets with Pulaski and introduces him to LaFayette and John Hancock. They talk about Pulaski's ideas for running a cavalry.

September 11, 1777—Washington convinces Congress to give Pulaski temporary command of the small, new cavalry detachment. On the same day, Pulaski saves military supplies and pushes the British back in a battle at Brandywine.

September 12, 1777—He prevents a surprise British attack at an area called Warren's Tavern.

September 15, 1777—Congress acknowledges Pulaski's leadership and bravery and decides to commission him as Brigadier General and give him command of four light cavalry regiments.

October 4, 1777—Washington honors Pulaski for his bravery and bold tactics after a skirmish with British General Howe's army at Germantown.

November 1777 to January 1778—During the winter at Valley Forge, Pulaski wants to train the cavalry properly, but is instructed by Congress to rest his men during the winter, as was customary at the time.

February 24, 1778—Pulaski's favorite horse is shot out from under him during a small battle at Cooper's Ferry. Although upset, Pulaski does not waste any time. With military dignity he quickly mounts another horse and continues to fight.

February 25, 1778—Frustrated that his cavalry has not been involved in any important battles, Pulaski decides to resign, but soon changes his mind when he comes up with a new idea. He asks Washington to start his own legion. He offers to recruit the men, outfit them, and train them in his own way. He would prepare this cavalry for active duty. After many convincing letters from Pulaski, Congress finally agrees. With 68 horses and 200 foot soldiers, the Pulaski Legion would become the Colonists' first true fully-trained fighting cavalry.

March to October 1778—Pulaski recruits many men, some Europeans and some Americans. At first, several of the American soldiers do not like him because he does not speak English, but once they see him in battle, they learn to respect his courage and intelligence.

May 17, 1778—After many months of tireless training and learning the finest European battle strategies, the cavalry is ready for battle—outfitted with new supplies purchased with Pulaski's own money. Pulaski's Legion is presented with their own battle flag made by the Moravian Sisters of Bethlehem, Pennsylvania.

October 8, 1778—A surprise attack is planned at Egg Harbor, New Jersey. The British find out about it and the Colonists lose many men. Although the raid is not a success, Pulaski's cavalry is able to get British supplies and hit 20 boats with artillery.

November 1778 to February 1779—Pulaski's Legion spends the winter in Minisink, New Jersey. The cavalry protects settlers from Indian attacks while awaiting orders for battle in the spring.

February 8, 1779—Pulaski is pleased to receive orders to join Benjamin Lincoln's forces in South Carolina and Georgia. When he and his men arrive in Charleston in March, the city is on the verge of surrendering to the British. Appearing before the City Council, Pulaski is able to convince the leaders of the city to reject the British ultimatum. Upon leaving the council chambers, Pulaski leads an attack that forces the British to abandon the Charleston siege. Charleston is saved, but Pulaski loses many men in battle.

October 9, 1779—Pulaski leads a heroic charge in Savannah, Georgia. When the battle is over, Casimir Pulaski is found severely wounded on the battlefield.

October 11, 1779—Pulaski dies while on the American brig *Wasp*. His body is buried at sea, and a symbolic funeral is held three days later in Charleston.

November 11, 1779—Washington orders that the password "Pulaski" be used that day and the response be "Poland" in honor of Casimir Pulaski, the Father of the American Cavalry.

Pulaski Remembered

Casimir Pulaski is remembered in many ways. In Poland, he is remembered as a man who fought for freedom on two continents. He was given the title "Soldier of Liberty." In addition, there are great celebrations held each year in Poland to honor Casimir Pulaski.

In the United States, many streets, bridges, counties, and towns are named after him. In Savannah, Georgia, there is a large monument remembering Pulaski. Since 1986, Illinois has designated the first Monday of every March as a state holiday in his honor. In fact, every year since 1929, the President has proclaimed October 11 as a memorial day in the United States in his honor. Above all, he is the man who provided the colonists with their first true legion on horseback. Casimir Pulaski is remembered as "The Father of the American Cavalry."

COUNT PULASKI.

Courtesy of POLISH MUSEUM OF AMERICA

35

Bibliography

Children's Titles

Abodaher, David, *Freedom Fighter: Casimir Pulaski*. New York: Messner Publishing, 1968. (Also published under the title *No Greater Love: Casimir Pulaski* by Copernicus Society of America, Philadelphia, Pennsylvania.)

Anderson, Sylvia and Riddle, Patricia, *Casimir Pulaski: A Polish American Hero*. U.S.A: Treehouse Publishing Company, 1987.

Adult Titles

Kopczewski, Jan Stanislaw, *Casimir Pulaski*. Warsaw, Poland: Interpress, 1980.

Szymanski, Leszak, *Casimir Pulaski: A Hero of the American Revolution*. New York: Hippocrene Books, Inc., 1994.

Other Books with Information on Casimir Pulaski

Army Times Editors, *American Heroes of Asian Wars*. New York: Dodd Press, 1968. (out of print)

Dictionary of American Biography. New York: Charles Scribner's Sons, 1964.

Lowenstein, Evelyn, et. al. *Picture Book of Famous Immigrants*. New York: Sterling, 1962. (out of print)

Madison, Arnold, *Polish Greats*. Boston: McKay Printing, 1980. (out of print)

Pilarski, Laura, *They Came From Poland: The Stories of Famous Polish-Americans*. New York: Dodd Press, 1969. (out of print)

Schultz, Pearle Henriksen, *Generous Strangers: Six Heroes of the American Revolution*. New York: Vanguard, 1976.

Sobol, Donald J., *Lock, Stock, and Barrel*. New York: Westminster, 1965. (out of print)

O R D E R   F O R M

	Price	Number	Cost
Stanley the Sleuth			
Uncovers the Story of			
Casimir Pulaski			
Hardcover edition, 40 pages.	$14.95	_____	_____
Coloring books, 40 pages, Paperback. (set of 8)	$9.95	_____	_____
Video tape, 11 minutes.	$14.95	_____	_____
Fifty Great Ideas to Celebrate			
Casimir Pulaski Day: A Teacher's Resource			
20 pages. Paperback.	$5.95	_____	_____
Casimir Pulaski: A Detailed Biography			
Ages 10-16, Paperback, 10 pages. (set of 10)	$8.95	_____	_____

subtotal _____

Please add 6.25% sales tax for Illinois orders. _____

Please add $2.75 for shipping and handling for the first book or set
and $1.00 for each additional book or set. _____

TOTAL _____

Send check or money order to: DanNaill Publishing
P.O. Box 92291
Elk Grove Village, IL 60009-2291

Name: _____

Attention: _____

Address:_____

City: _____State:_____Zip: _____

Phone number: _____
Schools or public libraries may use purchase orders or include tax exempt information.
P.O. # _____

Please allow 4 to 6 weeks for delivery.

Unconditional Guarantee!

At DanNiall Publishing we want our customers to be happy with their purchases. You may return any purchase at any time if you are not satisfied, and your full purchase price will be refunded, no questions asked.

Duplicate this form as necessary.

O R D E R   F O R M

	Price	Number	Cost
Stanley the Sleuth **Uncovers the Story of** **Casimir Pulaski**			
Hardcover edition, 40 pages.	$14.95	_____	_____
Coloring books, 40 pages, Paperback. (set of 8)	$9.95	_____	_____
Video tape, 11 minutes.	$14.95	_____	_____
Fifty Great Ideas to Celebrate **Casimir Pulaski Day: A Teacher's Resource**			
20 pages. Paperback.	$5.95	_____	_____
Casimir Pulaski: A Detailed Biography			
Ages 10-16, Paperback, 10 pages. (set of 10)	$8.95	_____	_____

subtotal _____

Please add 6.25% sales tax for Illinois orders. _____

Please add $2.75 for shipping and handling for the first book or set
and $1.00 for each additional book or set. _____

TOTAL _____

Send check or money order to: DanNaill Publishing
P.O. Box 92291
Elk Grove Village, IL 60009-2291

Name: _____

Attention: _____

Address:_____

City: _____ State:_____ Zip: _____

Phone number: _____

Schools or public libraries may use purchase orders or include tax exempt information.

P.O. # _____

Please allow 4 to 6 weeks for delivery.

Unconditional Guarantee!

At DanNiall Publishing we want our customers to be happy with their purchases. You may return any purchase at any time if you are not satisfied, and your full purchase price will be refunded, no questions asked.

Duplicate this form as necessary.